Keys to Vital Living

Understanding the Invisible Man

Keys to Vital Living

Understanding the Invisible Man

Alfred Ian Gunn-Russell

Take note that the name satan and related names are not capitalized. We choose not to acknowledge him, even to the point of violating grammatical rules.

Treasure House

An Imprint of

Destiny Image Publishers, Inc.®

P.O. Box 310

Shippensburg, PA 17257-0310

ISBN 1-56043-257-8

For Worldwide Distribution

Printed in the U.S.A.

Treasure House books are available through these fine distributors outside the United States:

Christian Growth, Inc.,
Jalan Kilang-Timor, Singapore 0315

Rhema Ministries Trading
Randburg, South Africa

Salvation Book Centre
Petaling, Jaya, Malaysia

Successful Christian Living
Capetown, Rep. of South Africa

Vine Christian Centre
Mid Glamorgan, Wales, United Kingdom

Vision Resources
Ponsonby, Auckland, New Zealand

WA Buchanan Company
Geebung, Queensland, Australia

Word Alive
Niverville, Manitoba, Canada

Dedication

This book is dedicated to my wife, Helen, given to me by God to join me in a ministry of pastoral counseling to people with problems.

To the Lord we say, "Thank you, for the priceless privilege of being the recipients of your grace and healing. Please use this manual to clear away the mists that the enemy has thrown around this subject and lead all who read it to a clear understanding of the enemy's wiles and Your marvellous plan of blessing and salvation."

Contents

Foreword

Are you a Christian doctor with a patient whom you have treated medically without improvement? Perhaps *this* book is for you!

Are you a Christian counselor whose patient is not responding to you but continues to be fearful, depressed, and perhaps psychiatrically troubled? Perhaps this *book* is for you!

Are you a pastor frustrated by some members of your congregation who are in the grip of some addiction and you are tempted to refer them to a counselor whose counseling is based on Freudian, Jungian, or other secular psychology? This book *is* for you!

Are there "cracks" in your marriage that are about to split open irrevocably? This book is *for* you!

Are you a "yo-yo" christian, your life alternating between victory and defeat? This book is for *you*!

If any of these problems apply to you, this short book will give you the basic biblical principles and directions for recognising the enemy's oppression, and releasing you, or your counselees authoritatively from this grip, and bringing victory into your life, marriage, family and church.

Introduction

God, in His wisdom, laid down certain principles for us in the Old Testament. These principles are continued into the New Testament, and are designed for the physical, psychological, and spiritual welfare of mankind. Through this provision God demonstrates to us His great love for us all. If we break any of these principles, the resulting breakdown in harmony leads to a lack of health or wholeness in spirit, soul, and body.

This short handbook presents a synopsis of these biblical principles and the steps we can take to combat illness and promote complete health in spirit, soul, and body. *Keys to Vital Living* is not a comprehensive guide, but a practical approach to the provision God has set down in the Bible. A purely psychological approach fails to effectively deal with so many of today's problems. It is only when we are humble enough to follow the Maker's manual that we can achieve effective, whole, and vital life!

Chapter 1

The Nature of Man

In the Middle Ages the alchemist was obsessed with trying to find the "elixir of life" that would allow a human being to live forever. Not surprisingly, no alchemist ever found this elusive substance! Then, in the nineteenth century, came Darwin, who tentatively proposed an evolutionary process as a theory to explain the formation of living things. His theory was seized upon by Huxley, a zealous atheist who was well known in the British Ivy League academia. In his passionate quest to disprove the existence of God, Huxley succeeded in lowering man to the level of a superior animal. It is possible that without Huxley, who was described as "Darwin's Bulldog," the theory of evolution may never have "taken off" as it did.

As a result, the prevailing secular philosophy left man without a spiritual content. The developments in the medical world (which was increasing in chemical, biological, and technical advances at the same time), also tended to concentrate on the physical side of man. With this one-sided emphasis, man's physical nature seemed to naturally confirm the evolutionary sense that man was purely a materialistic entity responsible only to himself. Thus it stripped from man his formerly prevailing sense of divine purpose.

Freud and other secular atheists realized that the pendulum had swung too far. They attempted to construct an understanding of the non-material part of man, which the new evolutionary view seemed to purposely ignore. This "part" of man was obviously a very substantial component in his makeup and personality, and influenced his behavior.

Freud then proposed theories about the workings of mankind's subconscious mind, and about the important part the primitive instincts—particularly of sex and survival—play in behavior patterns. Many secular psychologists today do not accept Freudian theories in their entirety. What Freud did do was remind the medical profession that there is indeed a non-material part of man that influences his life and should not be ignored.

What are God's theories about this part of man? To find out we need to look at the Maker's manual, the Bible. There we will see what God has to say about the invisible part of this complex creature, *man*, and about the effect of the invisible on the visible man, his health, and his behavior. First, though, we must understand the nature of mankind.

What Is Man?

> *What is man, that Thou art mindful of him? and the son of man, that Thou visitest him? For Thou hast made him a little lower than the angels, and hast crowned him with glory and honour. Thou madest him*

to have dominion over the works of Thy hands; Thou hast put all things under his feet (Psalm 8:4-6).

In other words, man is not just a physical entity; he is a person, a wonderful unique part of God's creation.

Genesis 1:26 tells us, "And God said, Let *Us* make man in Our image...." Man was made to be a reflection of God Himself.

Genesis 2:7 indicates that "God formed man out of the dust of the ground" (i.e., the physical part of man's being), "and breathed into his nostrils the breath of life; and man became a living soul" or being. Man became *a real person, conscious, with full ability to think, understand, and reason.*

In the New Testament we have more information about the parts of man. Paul says, in First Thessalonians 5:23, "...I pray God your whole spirit and soul and body be preserved blameless...." Notice the order of his words. When we talk of the parts of man we usually say "body, soul, and spirit." God's order of importance is "spirit, soul, and body." First Corinthians 15:45 states, "...The first Adam was made a living soul; the last Adam [Jesus Christ] was made a quickening [life-giving] spirit."

Hebrews 2:6-12 quotes Psalm 8, then points to Christ as the perfect man to whom God has given total control and dominion over all of creation.

Thus the Bible recognizes three distinct parts of man:

1. Body—the physical
2. Soul—the psychological
3. Spirit

Here we will look at the basics of man's body.

The Body

Through his physical body man can see, hear, feel, taste, and speak. It is also through his body that he can be seen, heard, and felt. What a marvelous thing the body is!

We can separate the body even further, with our minds, into flesh, bones, and fluids, of which the most important is the blood. Leviticus 17:11 states, "For the life of the flesh is in the blood...." In other words, the body depends upon the blood flowing through its arteries and veins for its very life. If you stop the blood from flowing, unconsciousness will follow. Continue to stop the flow and death occurs. We may study the body's anatomy and wonder at its intricate detail of skin, muscles, nerves, and blood and lymph vessels. We may

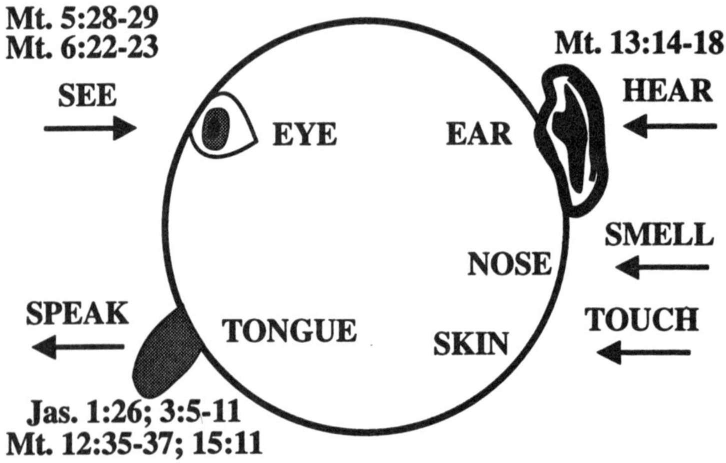

Figure 1: The Body

also think of it physiologically, with all its various functions of touch, taste, digestion, vision, hearing, smelling, and the ability to speak, perform exercise, and procreate.

Jesus told His disciples to be careful what they spent their time looking at (see Lk. 11:34-36). This warning has never been as important as it is today. We find ourselves bombarded on every side with films, cable TV, videos, "Dial-a-porn," and even pornography through the computer! All these media forms portray violence, sexual promiscuity, and perversion. As people allow themselves to watch these things, they dull their sensitivities. *What we see goes beyond the eye to the mind, heart, and will.* Jesus mentioned this truth in Matthew 5:28: "But I say unto you, That whosoever looketh on a woman to lust after her hath committed adultery with her already in his heart."

Thy Whole Body Shall Be Full of Light

> *The light of the body is the eye: if therefore thine eye be single, thy whole body shall be full of light. But if thine eye be evil, thy whole body shall be full of darkness...* (Matthew 6:22-23).

In other words, what we look at affects our thinking. This is especially so if we more than glance at something. We can spend our time gazing at it and fondling it in our minds until it has pervaded us with darkness. We may not even realize that it is darkness, and instead compliment ourselves on our "broad-mindedness." The fact is, impure sights produce impure thoughts, which produce impure actions.

Parents sometimes put their young children in front of a television set to keep them quiet without censoring what those children are watching. If these parents would stop for a moment to consider the frequency of violence, murder, and explicit sex that appears on these television programs, they would surely want to remove them from their children's viewing diet. Parents need to realize that what they are feeding into their children's subconscious mind is building a foundation for all their future behavior.

What is the alternative? Jesus said we were to look at what would have a good effect on our mind and life. Especially, "Let us fix our eyes on Jesus, the author and perfecter of our faith, who for the joy set before Him endured the cross, scorning its shame, and sat down at the right hand of the throne of God" (Heb. 12:2 NIV). This verse gives us one of the most life-transforming views we can have. If it involves belief and commitment, it will produce peace of mind and total confidence in God.

But Blessed Are Your Eyes, for They See...

> *But blessed are your eyes, for they see: and your ears, for they hear* (Matthew 13:16).

It has been said that the eyes are the mirrors of the soul. They frequently are! Our eyes can reflect alertness, joy, and peace—or deadness, dullness, tiredness, and hopelessness.

Some years ago Helen and I had a day conference on the Holy Spirit for students from Edinburgh University. During lunchtime Helen spoke to a group of six girls with lackluster eyes. When she asked them about themselves, she found out that all six girls were ministers' daughters and that all six were studying psychology. They also all had Marxist tutors whose teaching had undermined their faith! Your ears are almost as important as you eyes. (I say "almost" because we remember more of what we see that what we hear.)

...And Your Ears, for They Hear

> *But blessed are your eyes, for they see: and your ears, for they hear* (Matthew 13:16).

We live in a world that is filled with noise. The current trend for young people to run around with radios and CD players at full blast is causing a hearing loss in the same way workers in a steel factory become deaf to the sounds of the works. Such workers can hear each other talking without raising their voices, while a visitor hears nothing but the clanging of machinery!

In the Old Testament the boring of a hole in one ear *symbolized* the willing servitude of a servant to a good master whom he did not want to leave. We must beware what we hear! Most of the time we have a choice about what we hear. We must avoid feeding our minds through our ears with the unsavory, immoral things around us. "He that hath ears to hear, let him hear" (Mt. 11:15).

We need to beware *how* we hear as well. Perhaps we sometimes cannot avoid hearing bad, unsavory, and negative things, but we can avoid allowing them to linger in our minds. It is possible for us to turn off our radio and TV sets!

Heavy rock music can have an hypnotic effect upon people and, in the right surroundings, can produce a trancelike state. The heavy beat is similar to the jungle beat used for war or animistic worship, which is demon worship. Heavy rock professionals recognize and use this effect on themselves and on their audiences to produce a state of mass hysteria in worship of their idol (that is, the star singer). Remember—hiding behind every idol is a demon, and God has said, "Thou shalt have no other gods before Me" (Ex. 20:3).

As Christians, we must understand what happens when we allow young people, especially children, to listen to a daily diet of such music. Some of these secular groups are blatantly satanic; their songs are designed to change the moral standards of a whole generation and to divert worship from God to satan. More insidious still is the subliminal tracking used by many groups to foster promiscuity, drug use, rebellion, sexual perversion, and even satanism itself. Subliminal tracks are recordings below the level of conscious hearing. The messages are not consciously heard, but enter the subconscious mind and influence the thinking and moral values of the hearer. The ex-recordist for the Beatles personally told us that the recording George Harrison made many years ago, "My Sweet Lord," carried at least 12 tracks. The second track was faint, while the other ten were not consciously heard. Nevertheless they were very effectively fed into the subconscious of a whole generation. What happened? Promiscuity, rebellion, and anarchy exploded in society.

Many groups use this method to manipulate their audiences. Second Timothy 3:1-4 gives a very up-to-date picture:

> *This know also, that in the last days perilous times shall come. For men shall be lovers of their own selves, covetous, boasters, proud, blasphemers, disobedient to parents, unthankful, unholy, without natural*

affection, trucebreakers, false accusers, incontinent, fierce, despisers of those that are good, traitors, heady, highminded, lovers of pleasures more than lovers of God (2 Timothy 3:1-4).

The Tongue...a World of Iniquity

James 3:5-9 tells us about the tongue. It states that the tongue is "a world of iniquity" and "it defileth the whole body." These other Scriptures also tell us about what we speak with our tongue:

...Every idle word that men shall speak, they shall give account thereof in the day of judgment. For by thy words thou shalt be justified, and by thy words thou shalt be condemned (Matthew 12:36-37).

Not that which goeth into the mouth defileth a man; but that which cometh out of the mouth, this defileth a man (Matthew 15:11).

But those things which proceed out of the mouth come forth from the heart; and they defile the man. For out of the heart proceed evil thoughts, murders, adulteries, fornications, thefts, false witness, blasphemies (Matthew 15:18-19).

Joan was a very disturbed girl; she had a bad case of anorexia, went through bouts of severe bulimia accompanied by an obsession for shaving off her hair. She was a pretty girl and anxious to be free from her obsessions and suicidal urges. Upon counseling it was uncovered that one day when she was young, she was looking at herself in a mirror. Her mother walked past and said to her, "How come I got such an ugly child?" It was probably said in fun, but that remark was to color and destroy Joan's life until Jesus Christ set her free.

We must never underestimate the hearing and perception of children. They have minds that soak up anything and everything related to them. The Bible says, "Who hath ears to hear, let him hear," and "...blessed are your eyes, for they see: and your ears, for they hear" (Mt. 13:9,16). What we hear, what we see, and what we say all have an immense effect on both ourselves and others. What a young child sees and hears is of tremendous importance in forming true values in later life. The present rate of suicides among teenagers in America is a direct result of the deliberate lack of teaching of moral standards in school.

Touch and Smell—Other Important Senses

A baby thrives so much better if it is touched, caressed, and nursed in close contact with its mother and father. If a child has little loving contact with his parents, he may be left with an aftermath of rejection and lack of self-worth for the rest of his life.

Smell is another part of the consciousness that can discern good and bad. A pleasant smell will normally be healthy while an unpleasant smell can denote something bad or rotting. A demonically-affected site or situation can carry a peculiar smell all its own. Consider the odor in castle dungeons and other such places.

Chapter 2

The Soul and the Spirit

Soul

"And the Lord God formed man [his body] of the dust of the ground, and breathed into his nostrils the breath of life; and man became a living soul"...or being or personality (Gen. 2:7). Our word *psyche*, which we use in *psychology* and *phychosomatic* is a direct derivative of the Greek word for "soul." In this verse it means a living person, or being. There are three parts of the soul that the Bible talks about: (a) the mind, (b) the heart, and (c) the will.

I. The SOUL is the person, the "me" (Gen. 2:7).

   A. The MIND is the "psyche" (Gk. *psuche*). It includes the intellect, the memory, and the "computer" or reasoning of man (Rom. 1:28; 12:2).

   B. The HEART is the innermost being, the center of the conscious being, and holds man's intents and feelings (likes/dislikes).

C. The WILL is the active part of the soul; it translates reason and emotion into action (in the body). Or, in the court of the soul, reason and emotion present the case to the will, which then decides what to do. In this case, the independent witness is the conscience (in guilt). It is the God-given advocate for truth and righteousness.

Access to and from the soul to the world around is through the body—eyes, ears, mouth, nose, and skin.

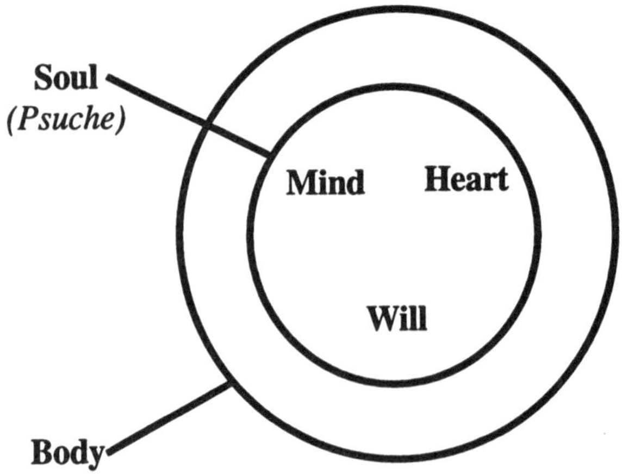

Figure 2: Soul *(Psuche)*

The Mind

The mind is the center of thought, reason, intellect, and memory. It is, if you like, the computer part of man. Here are stored all the memories of the past—both good and bad. Those who do not like the idea of God He gives over to a reprobate mind. "Moreover, since they considered themselves too high and mighty to acknowledge God, He allowed them to become the slaves of their degenerate minds, and to perform unmentionable deeds" (Rom. 1:28 Phillips). On the other hand, to those willing to be transformed by the renewing of their minds, God gives the opportunity of experiencing His good, acceptable, and perfect will (see Rom. 12:2).

The Heart

The heart does not refer to the bundle of muscle that pumps blood through our bodies, but to the center of our being. It is the heart in the same sense that we talk about the heart of a tree, the medulla, the strong central part, firm and able to withstand wind and weather. Here we find our emotions. Here is the innermost part of our soul, the center of our likes and dislikes and our deepest motivations and absolute beliefs.

Many Scriptures talk about man's heart. "For as [man] thinketh in his heart, so is he" (Prov. 23:7a). The heart controls the man. "Keep thy heart with all diligence; for out of it are the issues of life" (Prov. 4:23). It directs our lives, and therefore God has other important things to say about our heart:

> *And thou shalt love the Lord thy God with all thine heart...* (Deuteronomy 6:5).

> *Blessed are they...that seek Him with the whole heart* (Psalm 119:2).

> *Trust in the Lord with all thine heart...* (Proverbs 3:5).

> *A good man out of the good treasure of his heart bringeth forth that which is good...* (Luke 6:45).

> *For with the heart man believeth unto righteousness* (Romans 10:10a).

> *But those things which proceed out of the mouth come forth from the heart...* (Matthew 15:18).

The Will

The will is the "active" ingredient of the personality; it is responsible for putting into action the reasoning of the mind and the desires, longings, and inclinations of the heart. Our will decides on a course of action from what our reason and emotions say. The will decides what we gaze at, what we listen to, what we eat, what we drink, what we say, and even how we say it. Mixed into this decision-making process is also our conscience. To our peril we often resent, sometimes suppress, gag, or otherwise silence our conscience. In the Christian's beliefs, the conscience is a God-given monitor that helps guide us in our decisions.

From all this we see that influences—good and bad—gain entry to our mind and emotions through our five sense: seeing, hearing, smelling, tasting, and touching. At the same time, we influence our environment by what comes out of our heart and mind through our tongues.

Psychosomatic factors occur in 80 to 90 percent of all non-traumatic illnesses that physicians in general medical practices see. Some might dispute this figure, but I believe it to be near the mark. "Psychosomatic" merely indicates that the psyche, the biblical soul, influences the *soma*, or body, through stress, tension, or anxiety. David, the writer of most of the psalms said that we are "fearfully and wonderfully made" (Ps. 139:14). The truth of this statement becomes clearer with each new medical discovery that explains and illuminates the interactions taking place between the different parts of man!

Take a look, for a moment, at Figure 3.

Figure 3: Conscious & Unconscious

Both the conscious and the unconscious have parts to play in man's makeup. At the peak of the iceberg is this present moment—where we observe, listen, think, consider, and worry; feeling by both touch and emotion happiness, pleasure, sorrow, regret, and remorse. The submerged part of the iceberg is the record of the past—memories of facts, acts (ours and others), feelings, hurts, and attitudes. Again, these memories are both good and bad. It also stores past thoughts, emotions, learned reflexes, and reactions.

We could say that our present is the summation of our past. Although we can only recall a limited amount of the past at any particular time, the rest is not forgotten. It is only submerged, and can be resurrected from the depths given the right opportunity. Jesus said, "...every idle word that men shall speak, they shall they give account thereof in the day of judgment" (Mt. 12:36).

Secular psychoanalysis is concerned with digging out past factors that may be playing a part in feeding a present illness. We can understand that it is just as possible for God to bring to mind all the things we hope no one else knows.

The Spirit

Where is the spirit of man? What is the spirit of man? What is its interaction with the other parts of man? Can the spirit be distinguished? The answers to these basic questions are fundamental to understanding the whole nature of man.

1. Where Is the Spirit of Man?

We know from First Thessalonians 5:23 that man does have a spirit. That it is closely associated with the soul is clear from Hebrews 4:12, which states that the Word of God is sharp and powerful, "piercing even to the dividing asunder of soul and spirit, and is a discerner of the thoughts and intents of the heart." It is thus a definite entity in the non-material part of man. The Bible does not say anything about the site of the spirit.

2. What Is the Spirit of Man?

The spirit is the part of man that appreciates God—in fear, desire, apprehension, and love. Later we shall see the effect our environment has on our spirits.

3. What Is Its Interaction With the Other Parts of Man?

Through the spirit man responds to God and receives from God what God wants him to know and do, as well as what God wants him to impart to others. Before a person accepts Jesus as Savior, the spirit of that person is in a state of deadness. When the person does receive Jesus as Savior, God works in his life to produce a new creation. Jesus describes this as being "born again." Man's spirit is "quickened"; it becomes aware of and sensitive to God's will for him.

4. Can the Spirit Be Distinguished?

Some consider the spirit to be almost synonymous with soul. I believe it to be a separate entity. (Consider Hebrews 4:12.) Body (*soma*) and spirit (*pneuma*) can be separated, while spirit (*pneuma*) and soul (*psuche*) can only be distinguished (Cremer).

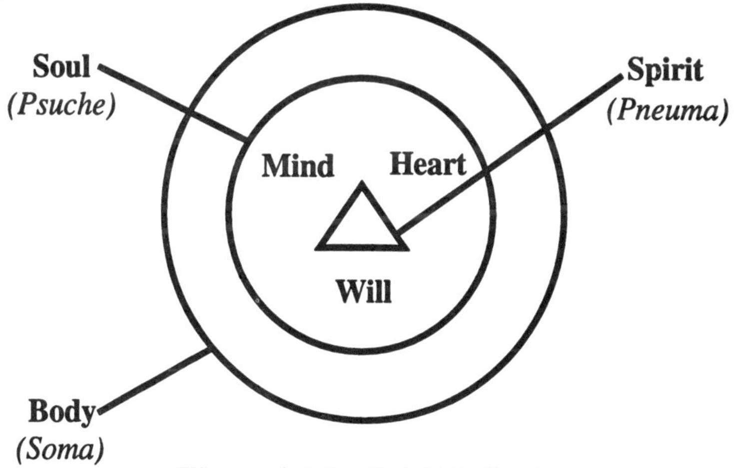

Figure 4: The Spirit & Soul

In summary, the body communicates with the world around it. The soul communicates with the world through the body and is aware of God by the spirit. The spirit's part is to communicate and bring us into tune with God. Our spirit is in a state of deadness until we have been born from above (see Jn. 3:3-8) by the breath of God (spirit, Gk. *ruach*, *pneuma*, meaning "breath").

Chapter 3

Whose World?

Who is in control of the kingdoms of this world at this moment? What is the nature of this ruler's authority? How did this state of affairs come about?

In order to answer these questions we must go back to the Word of God.

> *And the devil, taking* [Jesus] *up into an high mountain, shewed unto Him all the kingdoms of the world in a moment of time. And the devil said unto Him, All this power will I give Thee, and the glory of them: for that is delivered unto me; and to whomsoever I will I give it* (Luke 4:5-6).

The devil here claimed that he had been given dominion over the kingdoms of the earth. Notice that Jesus did *not* contradict him. Somewhere and sometime in the earth's history, satan obtained authority and was still in possession of it!

> *And God said, Let Us make man in Our image, after Our likeness: and let them have dominion over the fish of the sea, and over the fowl of the air, and over*

> *the cattle, and over all the earth, and over every creeping thing that creepeth upon the earth* (Genesis 1:26).

Here we are privileged to listen in to the highest decision-making meeting possible: God says, "Let *Us* make man...and let *them* have dominion!"

The Privilege and Responsibility of Authority

To Adam was given the unique privilege and responsibility of authority over the earth and all the animals. What a position! The man had the animals paraded before him and he named them one by one. At evening each day the Lord God walked and talked with man. It is a picture of perfection, completed when God gave Adam a woman as a companion and helpmate. God had given Adam the entire Garden to enjoy, but warned him not to partake of the fruit of the tree in the midst of the Garden. If he did so, he would die. However, danger lurked nearby. One day the devil, in the form of a beautiful serpent, met the woman as she walked alone in the Garden. He persuaded her to eat the fruit in order to be like God, knowing good and evil.

> *And when the woman saw that the tree was good for food, and that it was pleasant to the eyes, and a tree to be desired to make one wise, she took of the fruit thereof, and did eat, and gave also unto her husband with her; and he did eat* (Genesis 3:6).

We all know the rest of the story. First came the *thought of doubting God*, then a *blatant lie* about God, coming to a climax in a *rebellious act* by one and then the other. What happened? At that moment Adam handed over the dominion that God had invested in him to a usurper; thereby following the devil's lie rather than God's truth. It is rather like the "power of attorney," which is a person giving complete power over his affairs to a lawyer or a trusted friend in his absence. In the same way Adam handed over to his enemy, satan (which means adversary), the authority to use and thus misuse the dominion given to man.

This act had far-reaching consequences not only for Adam, but for the whole human race. Second Corinthians 4:4 states, "...the god of this world hath blinded the minds of them which believe not, lest the light of the glorious gospel of Christ, who is the image of God, should shine unto them." The blindness that started in Eden has continued to blind and pervert the human race ever since.

Paul calls satan the "god of this world" in Second Corinthians 4:4. In Ephesians 2:2 he says, "Wherein in time past ye walked according to the course of this world, according to the prince of the power of the air, the spirit that now worketh in the children of disobedience." There he uses the phrase "the prince of the power of the air" and "the spirit that now worketh in the children of disobedience."

Satan has many names:

- "the god of this world"
- "the prince of the power of the air"
- satan—adversary
- *diabolos*—(the devil); the accuser who slanders (Rev. 12:10)
- lucifer—shining one (Is. 14:12)

- beelzebub—prince of demons, or from "baalzbub" Old Testament Hebrew, lord of the flies; putrifier (Lk. 11:15)
- wicked one, sowing discord and confusion (Mt. 13:25,39)
- father of lies (Jn. 8:44 NIV)

Satan has a number of activities:

1. Satan opposes. "For our struggle is not against flesh and blood, but against the rulers, against the authorities, against the powers of this dark world and against the spiritual forces of evil in the heavenly realms" (Eph. 6:12 NIV).
2. Satan inspires lies. "The coming of the lawless one will be in accordance with the work of Satan displayed in all kinds of counterfeit miracles, signs and wonders" (2 Thess. 2:9 NIV).
3. Satan controls the disobedient. "In which you used to live when you followed the ways of this world and of the ruler of the kingdom of the air, the spirit who is now at work in those who are disobedient" (Eph. 2:2 NIV).
4. Satan accuses. "Then I heard a loud voice in heaven say: 'Now have come the salvation and the power and the kingdom of our God, and the authority of His Christ. For the accuser of our brothers, who accuses them before our God day and night, has been hurled down' " (Rev. 12:10 NIV).

But the Word says:

I will not speak with you much longer, for the prince of this world is coming. He has no hold on me (John 14:30 NIV).

And in regard to judgment, because the prince of this world now stands condemned ("has already been judged," Rotherham) (John 16:11 NIV).

That at the name of Jesus every knee should bow, in heaven and on earth and under the earth (Philippians 2:10 NIV).

For in Christ all the fullness of the Deity lives in bodily form, and you have been given fullness in Christ, who is the head over every power and authority (Colossians 2:9-10 NIV).

And I tell you that you are Peter, and on this rock I will build My church, and the gates of Hades will not overcome it. I will give you the keys of the kingdom of heaven; whatever you bind on earth will be bound in heaven, and whatever you loose on earth will be loosed in heaven (Matthew 16:18-19 NIV).

His intent was that now, through the church, the manifold wisdom of God should be made known to the rulers and authorities in the heavenly realms (Ephesians 3:10 NIV).

In spite of all satan's activity, however, God has decreed that the earth will one day be filled with the knowledge of the glory of the Lord (see Hab. 2:14). Jesus came to open eyes and turn people from darkness to light and from the power of satan to God (see Acts 26:18). When Jesus walked the earth, He had some very definite things to say about satan's rule:

1. "Now is the judgment of this world: now shall the prince of this world be cast out" (Jn. 12:31).

2. "...the prince of this world cometh, and he hath nothing in Me" (Jn. 14:30).
3. "...the prince of this world is [has already been] judged" (Jn. 16:11 Rotherham).

From these Scriptures we conclude that the coming of God's perfect Man brought to light the evil that was being perpetrated by the ruler of this world. Finding no point of weakness, sin, or response to his temptations in Jesus, satan was judged and would in a short time be cast out.

In Philippians 2:9-11, we see dominion being restored to the One who not only had the right by inheritance, but also earned it by His life of obedience and humility, and by His perfect sacrifice on the cross. Colossians 2:9-10 goes a step further and tells us that the total fullness of the Godhead dwells in the Lord Jesus Christ, and that *we*—the believers—are complete in Him. In other words, Jesus is *totally* supreme, even if most people don't see it. This authority Jesus shares with His Church (see Mt. 16:17-19). The only trouble is that the Church has not yet fully entered into the place of authority. I firmly believe that the time has come for the Church to step into that authority. God is waking His sleeping Church to its heavenly calling and responsibility, and as it comes of age and takes up its responsibilities, the principalities and powers in the heavens will see and know the supreme wisdom of God (see Eph. 3:10).

In Summary

In the beginning man surrendered his God-given dominion to a usurper, satan. Jesus then came into this world and defeated that usurper. He took from satan the power that he had been given by Adam. Jesus has taken back that authority and is in the process of teaching His Church (His children) to humbly take up their privilege of restored authority in Christ (*Yeshua*). This image of man in God's likeness was marred; the likeness degraded. His authority was given up by worshiping the usurper. *But* God is in the process of restoring the image, the likeness, and the authority to His real Church, the Body of Christ.

What effect then has satan's dominion on mankind? In John 10:10 we find the difference between the enemy's trademark and God's hallmark. A "trademark" on an article bears the maker's name, while a "hallmark" is the guarantee of tested purity of gold or silver. "The thief comes to steal, to kill, and to destroy" is the enemy's trademark! The Lord Jesus says, "I am come that you might have life and that you might have it more abundantly!" Satan steals peace, innocence, happiness, and joy. He kills our will to resist evil, if we let him, and then our bodies by the effects of his work. Finally, he desires to destroy our spirits eternally. How different is the hallmark of God's work in a believer—Life abundant with all its purity, beauty, and lasting joy.

Ever since satan usurped authority from our first parents by subterfuge, he has used it to try to denigrate God. He has tried to take God's place, and at the same time pervert and destroy man. Above all, he attempted to cut off the promised line of succession of God's appointed Deliverer who would crush his (satan's) head (see Gen. 3:15). Thus the world became a battlefield. After Eden, the conflict extended to Cain and Abel. With them the enemy was able to dispose of half of the succession. He then tried in Egypt, through Pharaoh, to kill all male babies and thus exterminate God's people. Again in Babylon through Haman he attempted to wipe out the Jewish people. When he heard that the Messiah had been born, he caused Herod to kill all the male children under two years old in Bethlehem. When he failed to eliminate Jesus at Bethlehem, the conflict extended itself to the wilderness, the cliff top at Galilee, the storms on the lake, and finally the assault at Calvary!

And so the battle rages on with us.

Chapter 4

The Battle Rages On

As soon as we are born we begin to die. Hugh Miller, a physiologist, once said, "Life is a slow process of death and death is bankrupt life." Satan's dominion over mankind began when Adam gave over his authority and sin began to reign. Its effects on mankind are seen in (a) the physical, (b) the psychological, and (c) the spiritual aspects of man.

The Physical

Age: The aging process goes on inexorably; nothing the alchemist of the Middle Ages or the scientist of modern times has produced could halt the process. Eccesiastes 12:1-7 is still true—degeneration of the body cells still progresses. Skin becomes thinned and flabby. The senses are dulled and slowed. Interest is lost, and the fear of aging and death haunts man's steps throughout his life.

Infection: The microorganisms that were created to be part of the natural process are altered and now attack mankind. This is particularly true when the body's resistance is slow or its defense mechanisms have been sabotaged.

Cancer: This is growth out of control, or "cells in rebellion."

Stress and Anxiety: In my experience of 35 years of medical practice, the psychological element was involved in 80 to 90 percent of the patients I treated. Stress has been called the curse of modern life—and not without reason.

Trauma: Accidents, at home or in traffic, are usually due to anger, carelessness, or ignorance. Major culprits are poisons, including drugs, alcohol, tobacco, and misused medicines. Violence is another—reflecting anger, loss of temper, hate, and suicide.

We might summarize the effects of satan's work on the body by saying that it kills, steals, and destroys health, vitality, well-being, and the joy of living.

The Psychological

Satan's trademark—stealing, killing, destroying—is seen in the soul, or psyche, of man. (See James 1:14-15 AMP and Ephesians 2:2-3.) Note the progression of evil in the Garden of Eden:

First satan posed an apparently innocent question that sowed a doubt about what God said. In Eve's reply, a lie was added. Then satan followed up by casting doubt on God's integrity and goodness.

Finally, Eve changed from thought to action. She looked at the fruit, at how beautiful it was; she imagined how delicious it would taste. Above all she longed for the fulfillment of satan's promise that she would be like God, knowing good and evil. After Eve ate the fruit, she immediately longed for company in her transgression, and gave it to her husband. This progression has been reflected in man ever since.

First comes a thought or a lie. It results in disobedience, then guilt, which is quickly followed by fear, shame, and separation from the source of goodness (God). We might express it like this:

1. superficial thought (or feeling)
2. attitude (voluntary choice)
3. habit (continuing attitude)
4. bondage (involuntary or fixed state)

How subtly satan manipulates our thoughts and feelings—developing attitudes and habits until he has achieved a measure of control in those areas of our lives—mental, emotional, or physical. His aim is death. For those who do not know Jesus as Savior and Lord, it means sharing eternity with the devil and his evil angels. For those who are true Christians, he tries to produce deadness in their lives toward God; destroying their joy in the Lord, he produces fruitless and defeated Christians.

Progression to Death

We can find another scriptural example in the life of King Saul of the Old Testament. Look at First Samuel 18:6-7.

> *And it came to pass as they came, when David was returned from the slaughter of the Philistine, that the women came out of all cities of Israel, singing and dancing, to meet king Saul, with tabrets, with joy, and with instruments of musick. And the women answered*

one another as they played, and said, Saul hath slain his thousands, and David his ten thousands (1 Samuel 18:6-7).

Saul listened, accepted his own interpretation of the sayings, and chose envy and anger. As he continued being resentful, anger and hate took over. The evil spirit that came upon him when he had previously disobeyed God, returned and expressed itself in his violent trying to kill David. By this time God had left Saul to his own way and devices. Later, after Samuel died, Saul found himself facing the Philistines alone, without God and without Samuel, and he was afraid—even terrified (see 1 Sam. 28:5)!

In this satanically generated fear, King Saul became desperate. Disguising himself, he went to Endor to consult a witch. Then, from Samuel's own spirit he was given God's message that God had become his enemy and had given the kingdom to David because Saul had disobeyed, dishonored, and rebelled against God. Finally, he was told that he and his sons would die the next day. The progression was complete—envy, anger, hate, the evil spirit, murder, seeking advice from satan, loss of the kingdom, and death. (The last included not only himself, but also his line of succession.)

We can also think of Judas; his lust for money led him to steal, betray his Master, and in remorse commit suicide. Another example is Herod. Consumed by lust for his sister-in-law, he adulterously married her, imprisoned John the Baptist for reproving him, and then because of his pride, murdered him. Later the Emperor Caligula banished Herod to Gaul, where he died.

Whether we like it or not, in life there is a definite relationship between cause and effect. Where there is an effect or result, there is always a cause. Satan has had great experience down through the ages in manipulating man's depraved mind to accept his thoughts and start the evil slide through attitude, habit, and bondage to death.

Our Responsibility

Where does man's responsibility lie in all this? It lies in his will.

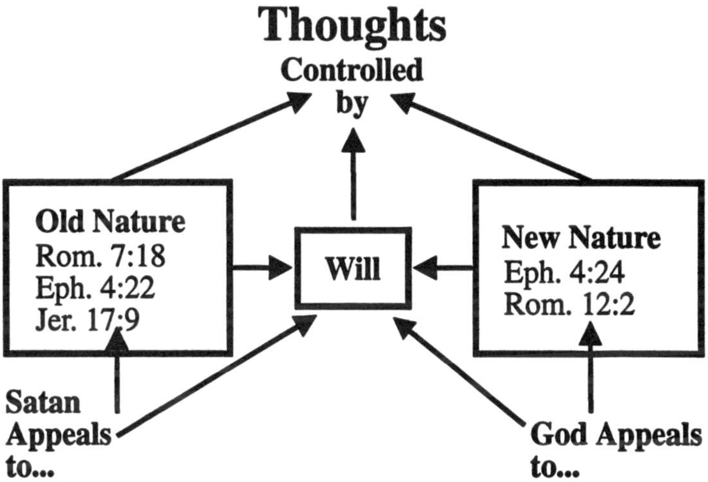

Figure 5: The Will

The will is at the center; it is responsible for what thoughts control our mind and what effects the old and new natures have on our thinking, and consequently on our actions or behavior.

Remember, the soul is primarily composed of the mind, or reason, and the heart (as in the heart of a tree or the heart of a matter) or emotions and the deep commitment and direction of our lives. The will is the arbitrator in the court of the soul; it decides what we say, do, and think.

It is our will that opens the door to outside negative factors—unforgiveness, resentment, bitterness, pride, rebellion, envy and jealousy, lies and deceit, lust and greed, self-pity, and doubt.

On the other hand, it is our renewed will that opens the door to the Holy Spirit, allowing Him to enter our conscious being to combat the effects of the powers of darkness.

How It All Works

The mind is the primary battlefield of the soul. Why? It is the target most easily available for satan to attack. The full effect of satan's dominion on the spirit of man is seen in Genesis 2:17: spiritual death, or alienation from God. Paul describes it as being "dead in trespasses and sins" (Eph. 2:1). The effect of the fall on man was death of spirit, soul, and body.

How does this effect us today as human beings? How does the progression of satan-assisted negativity occur? Because satan has the easiest access to our thought life with our inborn fallen nature, we tend to find sinful thinking, or thinking negatively much easier than thinking rightly or positively. In fact, there is an enjoyment in some evil thinking that satan then uses for his own ends. In the truly born-again believer, in the one who trusted in the Lord Jesus Christ for salvation, God has begotten a new nature. This reborn nature finds enjoyment in thinking good and positive thoughts.

A conflict then occurs between our old nature (see Eph. 4:22) and the new nature (see Eph. 4:24) in our thought life. Satan appeals to our old or fallen nature with all its lusts and enjoyment of negative thoughts, while God the Holy Spirit appeals to our new nature. Our thoughts may be our own, and be either positive or negative. Or they can be from the enemy as fiery darts (see Eph. 6:16) of doubt, confusion, and temptation to indulge in sinful thought or action. These thoughts could also be from God, to help us obey Him by thinking positive, good thoughts (see Phil. 4:8 AMP). Incidentally, it should be noted that many of the enemy's arrows can be presented to us as rational, reasonable, and desirable.

The will, the arbitrator, has the job of assessing our thoughts and deciding if they should be accepted or refused. The will is quite capable of functioning correctly until it is weakened by persistent, sinful, lustful, or negative thinking. Satan cannot hear our thoughts, but he can watch our eyes, expressions, and movements and so deduce the attitude of our thoughts fairly accurately. He can tell if we are following his leading. Figure 6 (next page) illustrates this progression of negativity. (See Appendix B for another view of this progression.)

Thoughts: "For as [a man] thinketh in his heart, so is he" (Prov. 23:7a). If we accept a negative thought—fondle it, enjoy it, allow it to become a regular visitor to our minds—it becomes an…

Attitude: An attitude, like a thought, is still subject to our will and can be changed voluntarily.

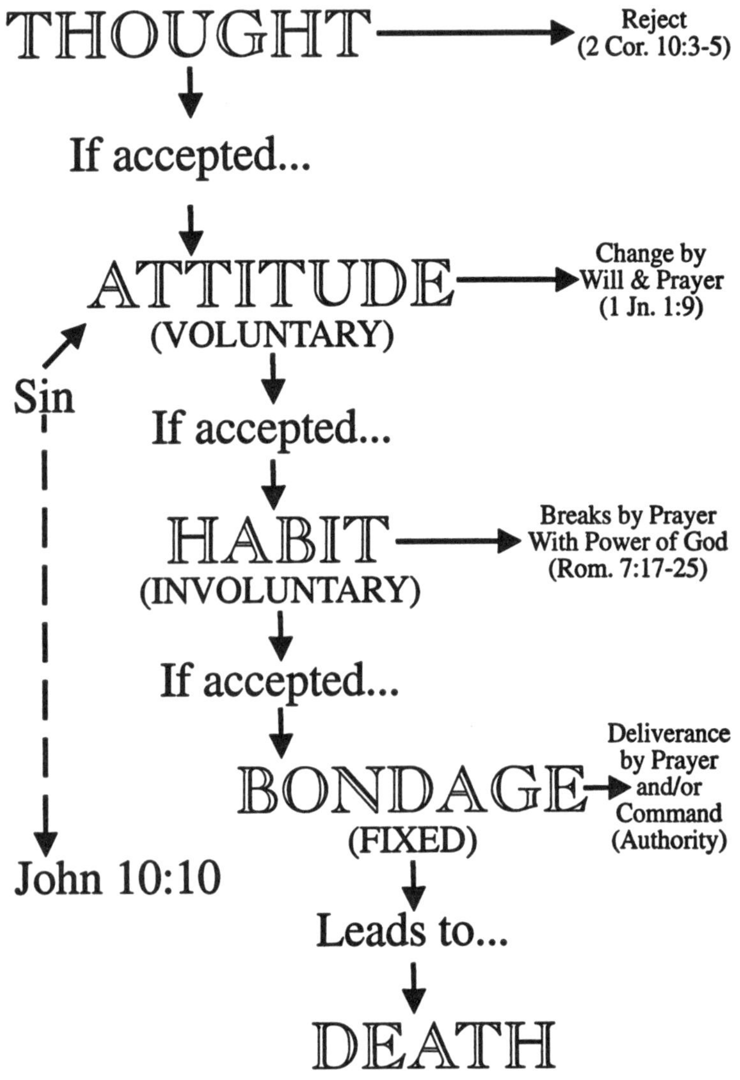

Figure 6: Progression of Negativity

Habit: If an attitude is accepted as normal and persisted in, it becomes a habit, or an obsession. This changeover is often unconscious and involuntary, and it is well nigh impossible for our wills to break it on their own. The negative or sinful habit is of course fostered and stimulated by satanic forces (i.e., demons).

Bondage: If we continue to submit ourselves to a sinful habit, we open ourselves up to demonic control and the habit becomes a bondage. This condition is beyond our capacity to reverse on our own. The eventual end result of this is death.

How good it is to know that God has an answer to each of these stages, or conditions! A sinful **thought**, instead of being accepted, can be refused and our minds brought into obedience to Christ (see 2 Cor. 10:4-5). Similarly we can use the shield of faith to quench all the fiery arrows of the evil one (see Eph. 6:16).

To refuse a sinful **attitude** we must be willing to refuse it by confessing it as a sin (see 1 Jn. 1:9), then claim God's power to turn from it. We need to do the same to refuse a sinful **habit**, claiming the victory won at Calvary by our Lord Jesus Christ (see Rom. 7:17-25). In this case, however, we will probably need the reinforcing prayer of one or two other mature Christians. I say "mature" because what comes into the open in counseling ministry is private; counselors must never succumb to the temptation to sin by gossiping.

A sinful **bondage** is a state of desperate need. A person in such a bondage may or may not be conscious of their need. If we know we are caught in such a state, we need to confess any known sin and claim the victory in the Lord Jesus Christ in the presence of one or two experienced Christians (this is very private). Plus, we need to renounce aloud the sinful bondage. Then one of those present ministering must take scriptural authority over the bondage and, if necessary, directly command any demonic spirit to leave in the name of Jesus. (We will examine this scenario more fully in a later chapter.)

The Spiritual

Whether we like it or not, we are in spiritual warfare as soon as we commit ourselves to follow the Captain of our salvation—the Lord Jesus Christ. He wants us to be strong in Him and able to stand against all the wiles of the enemy; thus He provides us with protection by giving us the use of His armor (see Eph. 6:10-18).

The warfare we are engaged is spiritual and is against satan's forces: fallen angels, the hidden (occult) powers of hell and darkness, and princes, authorities, and demons. Through them he is provided with a well-organized army. He attacks mankind in order to lead them to a Christless eternity with him. In particular he attacks and tries to defend himself against the power of God in and through the Christians engaged in spiritual warfare. (Note that satan is not omnipresent like God; he depends on his system of communications to know what is happening.)

We are not told, nor do we need to know, all about satan's shadow government in the Bible. We do know that he has princes with great powers over countries and that he has authorities controlling the interests of wickedness in organized evil on earth. His front line of attack on individuals is through demonic spirits. These have no bodies in which to express their desires and lusts. Thus they take every opportunity people knowingly or unknowingly give them to express themselves in lustful thoughts, attitudes, and habits of doubt, unbelief, lies, perversions, murder, adultery, and suicide. They continue their onslaught until they have produced a true bondage in people where the demons have free access to express the hateful work of their master at their will.

But the Lord Jesus Christ totally defeated satan in his own stronghold when He went into the tomb and came out victorious. Jesus has provided us with a complete set of armor for our warfare. He is also in the process of restoring our authority as the sons of the living God against all the power of the enemy. The Church has largely ignored its God-given authority, instead believing the devil's lies that its authority passed away with the apostles. Nowhere does the Bible suggest that the authority to cast out demons and heal the sick has been withdrawn. On the contrary, He has given His followers the authority of His name, Jesus, to use in the wisdom and power of the Holy Spirit, "to preach the gospel to the poor...to heal the brokenhearted, to preach deliverance to the captives, and recovering of sight to the blind, to set at liberty them that are bruised" (Lk. 4:18).

Chapter 5

What Can We Do?

As Christians, what can we do to promote positive health and strength of spirit, soul, and body? We must go to the Maker's manual, of course. That does not mean the secular, atheistic, humanistic philosophy of "being" as in secular psychology. Only the Maker knows the exact components of His creation. He has given us, if we are willing to see them, true psychological principles in the manual—the Bible! God has laid down principles for our body's behavior and health, our soul's behavior and health, and our spirit's behavior and health, which can enter into true *life* by a renewed relationship with its Maker.

Yahweh Rapha describes God in this relationship. *Yahweh* (*Jehovah*) is God's personal name as a holy, covenant-keeping God. *Rapha* describes an aspect of His being. It is not just that God heals, but His whole nature is to heal, make whole or save, whether spirit, soul, or body. God's whole being longs for us to be "whole." However, while God is sovereign in all His dealings, He will not override our free will. Nowhere is this more true than when we depict Christ knocking at the door of the human heart, seeking an invitation to come in as Savior and Lord. He will not enter as a thief, but only as a welcome guest.

Again we must remind ourselves of God's order of priority—spirit, soul, and body—when we minister to the needs and problems of people.

When promoting health of spirit, soul, and body, we retrace the same steps, but in a positive progression upward instead of downward. (See Appendix C for another view of this progression.)

As difficult as it is, we can bring our **thought** life under control by:

1. Casting down imaginations and bringing every thought into obedience to Christ (see 2 Cor. 10:5).
2. Training our minds to think and dwell on whatever is true, honest, honorable, just, right, pure, lovely or lovable, kind, gracious, excellent, virtuous or praiseworthy (see Phil. 4:8).

As we continue to keep our thoughts under control in the same spirit described in Philippians 2:5-8, the **attitude** of our mind becomes positively directed toward the only perfect life this world has ever seen: the life of the Lord Jesus Christ. Jesus said:

> *Abide in Me, and I in you. As the branch cannot bear fruit of itself, except it abide in the vine; no more can ye, except ye abide in Me. ...He that abideth in Me, and I in him, the same bringeth forth much fruit...* (John 15:4-5).

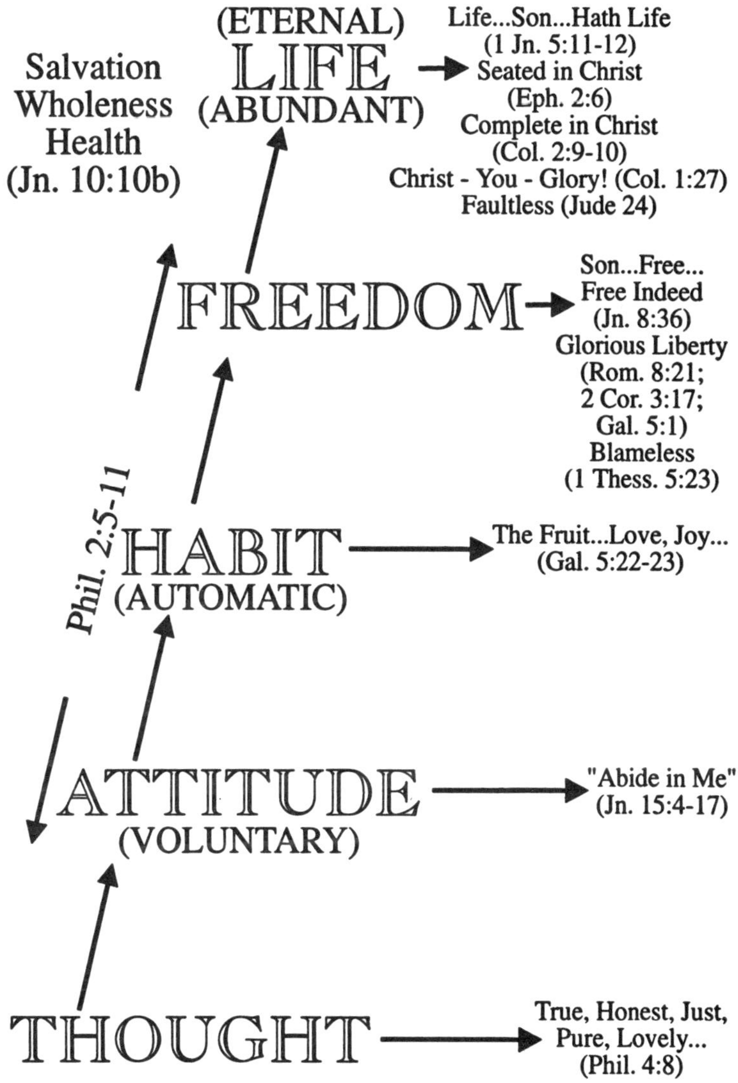

Figure 7: Positive Progression

Changing attitudes is voluntary; it requires perseverance on our part.

We are not robots; effort is required. Even Paul exhorted Timothy to fight the good fight. Abiding in Christ is not a passive state; rather it is one in which we encounter opposition from all the powers of darkness. In Romans 12:2 we read, "...be ye transformed by the renewing of your mind, that ye may prove [experience for yourselves] what is that good, and acceptable, and perfect, will of God."

Likewise, our old nature's thoughts will still trouble us whenever the opportunity presents itself. That is why Paul told the Colossians to "keep your mind set on things above" (see Col. 3:1-2). As we follow his instruction, we shall see our attitudes develop into habits of thought and action. Just as Jesus said that whoever lived, abode, and dwelled in Him would bear much fruit, so our **habits** are the fruit of a consistent attitude on our part.

As we abide in Christ and His word abides in us, the Holy Spirit produces goodness, uprightness of heart, and trueness (integrity) of life (see Eph. 5:9). Notice that it is the *Holy Spirit* who produces the fruit, not us. Ours is the attitude of abiding. The Holy Spirit produces fruit that glorifies God, pleases Him, speaks to others around us, and leads to the peace of God taking control of (ruling in) our minds (see Gal. 5:22-23). These positive habits then bring great **freedom** to us—freedom to enjoy the glorious liberty of the sons of God (see Rom. 8:21). All anxiety and stress take an appropriately minor place as we realize that God is in control and working all things together for good to those who love God and are called according to His purpose (see Rom. 8:28). "Free indeed" is how Jesus described it (Jn. 8:36).

The great liberation that God's freedom brings allows us to enter to fully enjoy the blessings He has for us as members of His family (Eph. 1:3-12).

We have eternal life now (see 1 Jn. 5:11-12). As we live through faith in Christ, and as we obey Him and put His words into action, He causes us to enjoy abundant **life** (see Jn. 10:10).

God views us as invested with Christ's righteousness now; it is given to us as a gift (see Rom. 5:17). We are seated in Him and complete in Him (see Eph. 2:6; Col. 2:9-10). The future is secure in Christ; at His future reception in Heaven's throne room He will present us faultless and with exceeding joy (Jude 24).

In Summary

Eternal life is ours the moment we put our trust in our Lord Jesus Christ, but the true enjoyment of eternal life comes to us to the extent that we follow, obey, and abide in Him.

In the battles of life, it is beyond price to realize that, as we abide in Him, we can truly say, "If God be for us, who can be against us?" (Rom. 8:31b)

The salvation that God gives us is much greater than most of us realize. This salvation includes our spirits being renewed and born again by the Holy Spirit—He begets within us His life, making us members of His family.

Our souls are being saved by the renewing of our minds, by a new heart (new desires), and by the sanctification of the Holy Spirit, unto holiness. Our bodies, which in the day to come will be both whole and holy (1 Jn. 3:2-3), can participate to some degree in wholeness now.

Wholeness comes, in a large part, from holy living. By this I do not mean "unco holy," as the Scottish poet might say, a false appearance of piety, but rather following and obeying God's rules in His manual, the Bible. After all, He gave them for our healthy and truly happy functioning as human beings. The Shorter Catechism puts it very well: "Man's chief end is to glorify God and enjoy Him forever." It is impossible to lead an abundant, fulfilled, and satisfying life if we are experimenting with the enemy's allurements and succumbing to his temptations to think, devise, express, and do evil. In fact, true abundant life is inhibited to the same extent we disobey God and do not glorify Him.

On the other hand, salvation is a free gift from God that is a result of the work of the Lord Jesus Christ on Calvary. God's desire for us is to experience His salvation and wholeness here and now, as we glorify Him.

Jesus' words in John 10:10b portray God's desire for us:

I am come that they might have life, and that they might have it more abundantly.

Chapter 6

A Synopsis of the Basics

Two realms of influence exist in the world: the seen and the unseen. This unseen realm can be good or evil. In it are two kingdoms—one of light and one of darkness. There are two kings: King Jesus (*Yeshua*), the Holy One of God; and prince lucifer (the shining one), the wicked sham.

Our world is the stage for a mighty cosmic conflict between these two powers, and whether we like it or not, we are involved. On the one hand the Lord Jesus Christ offers us full salvation—redemption, forgiveness of sins, cleansing from the defilement of sin, justification, sanctification, new birth, and the right to live in a new dimension of life through the Holy Spirit within, deliverance from the bondages of the enemy by the mighty power of God, and the right to live in victory as the sons of God.

On the other hand, satan, the adversary, opposes all that God does. He endeavors to keep his activities hidden so he can keep his power of manipulating mankind, individuals, and nations, working through deceit, disrupting peace, formenting unrest and wars, and producing opposition to God wherever he can. He keeps his activities shrouded in darkness; if his work is revealed, he loses his power to deceive.

Figure 8 shows some of the more common areas of satanic territory. God forbids His children to dabble in these because He knows that if they do, they will end up in misery—under the power of the enemy.

Don't Panic

It is important to keep a clear perspective on this situation; you want to avoid being overcome with fear. God has everything under control!

In Luke 11:20 Jesus said, "But if I with the finger of God cast out devils, no doubt the kingdom of God is come upon you." In other words, the finger of God is quite sufficient to deal with any demon!

In Isaiah 9:6 we read, "For unto us a child is born, unto us a son is given: and the government shall be upon His shoulder...." One shoulder of God is quite sufficient to take care of the government of the whole world.

In Luke 15:4-7 we read of the good shepherd who seeks the lost sheep who, when he finds it, puts it on his shoulders and brings it home rejoicing. What a marvelous picture of the loving care God takes with His own. How reassuring!

In Matthew 28:18b Jesus said to His disciples, "All power is been given unto Me in heaven and in earth." Then He says, "Lo, I am with you alway [every day], even unto the

2 REALMS	VISIBLE		
	INVISIBLE	Good	
		Evil	

2 KINGDOMS of LIGHT

of DARKNESS

2 KINGS

KING JESUS (*Yeshua*) The Holy One of God

PRINCE LUCIFER (Shining One)
Wicked Sham

OCCULT FORBIDDEN Lev. 19:31; 20:6-7; Deut. 18:10-15

(A) DIVINATION		
To Foretell the Future or Unknown	Astrology	Planet's Horoscope
	Hepatoscopy	Sacrifice Entrails
	Hydromancy	Pendulum
	Necromancy	Consult Dead
	Rabdomancy	Tea Leaves; Sticks & Arrows
	Mediums (Endor)	
	Fortune Tellers (Acts 16:16)	Palm, Ball, Tarot, Ouija
(B) SORCERY	**Magic**	Amulets
To Influence People or Events	Witchcraft < White / Black	Charms
		Spells
		Voodoo
	Mind Control	Dianoetics, Silva, etc.
	Spiritist Healing	
(C) SATANISM	**Direct Worship of Satan** (Total Will)	

Figure 8: The Occult

end of the world [to the end of time]" (Mt. 28:20b Rotherham). The One who is always with us is also the One who has *all* authority in Heaven and earth—and He has promised never to leave us or forsake us! (see Heb. 13:5)

Jan's Story

One evening two young ladies by the names of Jan and Sue arrived at our home in Scotland without knowing exactly why they had come. As usual, we finished the evening with prayer, and suddenly Jan told us how her 11-year-old daughter had developed a school phobia for the past year. She was unable to go to school, despite the help of a psychiatrist and medication. Nothing would persuade her to enter the gates of her school.

Jan was in her early thirties and had not been a Christian for long. We asked her about this. "When did you become a Christian?"

"Two years ago," she replied.

"Have you ever had your fortune told by palm reading?" we wanted to know.

"Oh yes!" she answered.

"When?" was our next question.

Her answer, "Three years ago!"

Then suddenly the Lord revealed the whole picture. She had gone into enemy territory by having her palm read, thus giving him a legal right to trouble her. He had not troubled about her while she was no threat, but as soon as she became a Christian, he attacked. His kingdom had been threatened.

So the enemy took up his options on her daughter, who developed a mysterious illness that produced a school phobia.

I said, "Now Jan, by going into enemy territory, it was as though you handed the keys of your mind or hereditary line over to Satan. On this occasion he took up his option on your daughter."

Jan said, "Well, what can I do about it?"

"First of all," I answered, "you must confess to the Lord that you had you palm read and you repent of that."

This she did and we laid hands on her and prayed for her daughter, claiming the Lord's healing. It was almost six months before she returned with her prayer group, including her rector, and told us and them what had happened that night after she left our home. When she had returned home, her daughter was asleep in bed, but awoke after Jan and her husband had gone to bed. Her daughter was in severe pain, and vomited and kept on vomiting for so long that Jan began to get really alarmed. She thought, *If this is the result of prayer, I am not quite sure if we should have prayed.* However, eventually the vomiting stopped and they all went back to bed exhausted. At 7:40 the next morning she was still sound asleep when into the bedroom bounded their daughter, "Quick, Mom, and Dad, it is time to get up! I shall be late for school if you do not get up now." Later, she emptied her pills down the sink, saying, "I will not be needing these any longer." She had no idea where her mother had been that night. Jan had confessed her sin. We had prayed together for her daughter. The Lord then annulled the enemy's option and healed her.

Answers to Common Questions

If satan's work is occult and hidden, how can we be aware of it?

One indication is changes in behavior, or varying behavior from time to time. The person may be irrational at times, or moody, or may blaspheme. This last may occur particularly if the name of Jesus is mentioned. Indeed the person may become quite violent at hearing Jesus' name, especially if it is used in prayer. Some of these changes may alert family or friends that all is not well. The person himself may not be aware of what he is saying or even doing, and might deny it.

How can satan gain access to a person?

A. Any involvement in the occult gives satan access.
   1. **Divination:** fortune-telling, palm reading, tarot cards, crystal ball
   2. **Sorcery:** witchcraft, influencing people or situations by spells or charms
   3. **Satanism:** joining a satanic church or attending one
   4. **Involvement in Cults:** either anti-God or anti-Christ philosophy; for example, Unitarianism, Luciferianism, Free Masonry, Eastern religions, Mormonism, Jehovah's Witnesses, etc. (Some of the more traditional sectors of the Church may have problems with idolatry in one form or another, which may also produce bondages.)

B. Involvement in sexual sins or extremes allow satan access.

- Sexual promiscuity
- Sexual perversions (sodomy, lesbianism)
- Sexual abuse (direct or as satanic ritual)

C. Addictions of any kind open a person to bondage to satan.
- Drugs
- Pornography
- Heavy metal or satanic music

D. Willful commitment to sinful thoughts can result in entrenched attitudes and bondages.

E. A demonic spirit can be introduced to a young child by a psychic parent wishing to provide for the child's future.

We ran into this situation in Scotland when a Free Presbyterian minister brought a very distressed and troubled young woman to see us. We ascertained that she had committed her life to the Lord, but bizarre behavior had continued. We talked to her about the Lord Jesus Christ and how we need Him to be in control of our lives, when suddenly she lunged forward, grabbed my tie, and pulled with all her might.

By the grace of God, the tie knotted instead of slipping up to choke me. It was clearly a case of a demonic presence, so I said firmly but not loudly, "What is your name?"

"Samantha!" came the answer.

I responded, "Samantha, I bind you, taking authority over you in the mighty name of Jesus, and command you to come out. Take your hands off Gloria and be gone to the place of the Lord's appointing."

The lady's whole face suddenly changed, bloated, filled with venom and hate as the demon realized that it had revealed itself. She vomited and slumped onto the floor, unconscious, where she remained for two or three minutes while we prayed over her. Then she sat up, fully conscious, and told us the rest of her past history.

Gloria was the seventh child of the seventh child of the queen of the Gypsies (Romanys) in Britain. By the time she was born, there wasn't anything left to bequeath to her. Thus they put into her, at birth, the spirit Samantha so she could support herself by telling fortunes. (Compare the story of Paul and the girl with the python spirit in Acts 16:16-18.)

If you are faced with such a disturbed person, there are a few questions you need to determine: Is this behavior from the old nature, or the old nature *and* demonic bondage? And if it is demonic, then is it *latent* (that is, are there any demons hiding nearby, trying to avoid detection) or is it *patent* (manifesting in some way)?

Can a Christian have a demon?

This is a thorny question for many people, particularly those who have not had to deal with the enemy in this area. There is no doubt that such a scenario is possible. In his classic *Demons in the World Today*, Dr. Unger came to the conclusion that a Christian could have a demon, and I agree. Yes, a Christian *can have* a demon, *but* a demon *cannot have* a Christian! The difference is vital.

How can this happen? Quite simply, it can be a carryover from preconversion days, particularly if pride has not been surrendered. Consider this simple illustration. Buckingham

Palace has, I believe, more than 400 rooms. Suppose a burglar breaks into a room on the ground floor. As long as he remains out of sight, as long as no one sees or hears him, he is left alone. He may even come and go as he pleases if no one notices him. However, as soon as he is discovered by guards or police, he is removed to jail and charged with breaking and entering. At no time would anyone suggest that the burglar possessed Buckingham Palace. The palace remains in the possession of the Queen.

Many people use the term *possessed* in relation to demons. This word does not occur in the Bible. The term it uses is *demonized*, or affected by a demon. If we use the word *possessed*, we immediately think of the demoniac of Gadarenes—and that can happen. However, when Jesus healed the woman with the bent back, He said satan had bound her for 18 years (see Lk. 13:16).

In a similar way, a demon could use us to express something negative for its own ends, particularly if we are not keeping our thoughts, feelings, or imagination under control. This is exemplified when Peter expressed horror that Jesus would let Himself be crucified. To that Jesus replied, "Get thee behind Me, Satan" (Mt. 16:23). Jesus recognized that it was not Peter, but satan, who was speaking.

Dealing With the Occult

Are you personally prepared for confrontation, should it arise? There are some things you need to have established first:

1. Are you secure in Christ?

2. Are you aware of your authority in Christ, and of your authority to use the name of Jesus?
3. Have you brought all your known sins to the Lord in confession, asking for forgiveness and the cleansing of the blood of Jesus?

The third one is very important because satan will look for anything he can use to counter our authority in Christ. In John 14:30b Jesus said to His disciples, "The prince of this world cometh, and hath nothing in Me [no hold over Me]." There the enemy could do no more than he had permission to do.

When you address a demon, you must address it authoritatively. You don't need to raise your voice, although sometimes that happens without thinking. You simply address it from your position as a child of the King—with authority and without fear. Every demon must bow in submission at the name of *Jesus*. If it is slow to go, just remind it of the blood of Jesus, which at once reminds it of your redemption and its eternal condemnation.

Finally, if you are asking someone a question whom you suspect may have a demon present, always use the *person's* first name. If you don't, you could get an answer from the demon. Such an answer would not be the answer the person wishes to give you because the demon, like its father the devil, is a liar.

A person who has been delivered from a demon or such bondages needs some follow-up care. The following Appendix is composed of a sheet we give to people after ministering to them in this way.

Appendix A

Aftercare: Spiritual Convalescence

So now you are set free from the restraints, constraints, and bondages that bound and perhaps tortured you. Isn't God good? He has delivered you from the kingdom of darkness and translated you into the Kingdom of His dear Son, and He wants you to live in spiritual victory as a son or daughter of the King. This is something new for you; you now have to learn how to behave as a child of the King.

The first thing you need to know is that the old enemy, satan, will not give up just because you escaped his grip. True, he no longer has the same power over you, but he will try to persuade you that he does! He knows your weaknesses and old thought and habit patterns, and will try to reestablish them if he possibly can. It is like the tracks that old farm wagons used to make on beaten earth roads. Those tracks gradually deepened with use until it was difficult to keep the wheels from slipping back into the old tracks.

Satan will try to reassert his control over you in any way he can, but do not be anxious—the Lord Jesus Christ has defeated him at Calvary and He wants you to live in the power of the victory He won for you there. How do we do that? Paul says in Second Corinthians 10:3-5 (NIV):

> *For though we live in the world, we do not wage war as the world does. The weapons we fight with are not the weapons of the world. On the contrary, they have divine power to demolish strongholds. We demolish arguments and every pretension that sets itself up against the knowledge of God, and we take captive every thought to make it obedient to Christ.*

Next we are given the spiritual armor in Ephesians 4:10-18. All the armor is needed; none can be left off. It means first that we must be men and women of integrity and truth. We need the girdle of truth; Jesus said, "I am the truth" (Jn. 14:6). We need the breastplate of righteousness, the helmet of salvation, and the firm shoes that give us secure footing when we are on God's business. These are the "fixed" pieces of armor God has given us. He also gives us two pieces of armor of great importance that are not strapped on, but must be handled. These are the shield of faith, given to us to quench all the fiery darts of the enemy, and the sword of the Spirit, which is the Word of God.

These two pieces of armor can be left lying on the ground where they don't do any good. We might call them the "active" pieces of armor, while the others, since they are fastened in position, we might call the "fixed" pieces of armor.

The active pieces are for us to use when occasion arises. Naturally the shield will not stop fire-tipped arrows if it is lying on the ground. No sword will put the enemy to flight if it is not in your hand.

You may ask, "What are fire-tipped arrows?" These arrows are tempting thoughts, feelings, or imaginations that the enemy tries to get you to accept as your own. After a session of deliverance, these fiery darts will assail you at your weak point. They will first be doubts that God indeed set you free from your old sins, failings, weaknesses, and habits. After shooting doubts at you, he will try to get you to accept fear, particularly of failure. He will attempt to make you afraid that God is not really able to maintain deliverance, and that you will surely return to your addiction—drugs, alcohol, sexual impurity, pornography, overeating, or overspending—or to your previous despondency or depression. His aim is to get you to accept these thoughts as your own and so reestablish his control over you.

Don't accept those thoughts! God has given you the authority to quench all such darts with the mighty shield of faith, and to put the enemy to flight with the sword of the Spirit—the Word of God. Jesus effectually used the "sword" when tempted by satan in the wilderness. He quoted Scripture and immediately each temptation came to an end. (See Matthew 4:1-11.) God has given us His Word to use in the same way and with the same result!

"Why does God allow me to be tempted like this?" you may ask. Before I answer, think what the word *tempted* means here. It could be translated as "tested," or "tried." A pupil is tested to see if he or she has learned what the teacher has taught. A soldier is put through "boot camp" for training before going into battle. He must be able to use his weapons automatically in warfare. In the same way God allows the enemy to "try" us, that we might learn to use the weapons He has given us and to gain confidence, through practice, in their effectiveness for defeating the foe. In other words, these attacks are to produce efficient, spiritual soldiers; prevent laziness; and teach us to use our spiritual authority over the enemy.

How do we do it? First, we recognize the origin of the thought or imagination. Is it from God, yourself, or the enemy? If it is from God, then it will be positive and good, and we will not doubt its source. Your thoughts, on the other hand, are not always as good as they should be. However, you do not need to go back to what you just left; you can change those thoughts. Thoughts from the enemy are always negative and doubting God. They will try to seduce you to return to the sin or weight from which you were just delivered.

When a thought from the enemy crosses your mind and you recognize it, you must lift your shield by refusing the thought, saying, "I refuse that thought in the all-powerful name of Jesus, who is my Lord. You have no authority over me. Romans 6:14 says, 'Sin shall not have dominion over you' and that means me because the Lord Jesus Christ is my only Lord and Master from now on!"

There are three things about Jesus I want to leave with you:

1. He has been given *all* power and authority in Heaven and on earth (see Mt. 28:18).
2. He will always be with us; He will never forsake us (see Mt. 28:20).
3. He loves you (see Jn. 15:9).

How good it is to be sure of His provision for us!

Finally, *read the Word* daily; *pray* with thanksgiving; and *obey Him* as He directs you through His Word.

Appendix B

Positive Progression

THOUGHT or FEELING	ATTITUDE (Volitional)	HABIT (Automatic)	HEALTH-SALVATION WHOLENESS HALLMARK (of God)		
Phil. 4:8	**Jn. 15:4-17**	**Gal. 5:22-23**			
True	**A**	Love	Christ in You - Glory		**A**
Honest	**B**	Joy	(Col. 1:27)		**B**
Honorable	**I**	Peace	Blameless	**L**	**U**
Noble	**D**	Longsuffering	(1 Thes. 5:23)	**I**	**N**
Just	**E**	Gentleness	Seated in Christ	**F**	**D**
Pure		Goodness	(Eph. 2:6)		
Lovely		Faith	Complete in Christ	**E**	**A**
Kind	**I**	Meekness	(Eph. 4:12-13,16,23-24		**N**
Good	**N**	Self-Control	Faultless		**T**
Gracious			(Jude 24)		
Praiseworthy	**M**	Humility			
	E	Patience			
		Forgiving			
		Loving			